The Twelve Seasons of
VERMONT

The Twelve Seasons of
VERMONT

Photographs by
Vermont Life Contributing Photographers

Text by
A Selection of Vermont's Finest Writers

A Vermont Life Book

MONTPELIER, VERMONT

(handwritten note in left margin) DWL <Burlington Diversity Day 5/5/2005 .the panelists gift

COVER: *Fall in Peacham. Photograph by Merlin Lacy.*
PAGE 2: *Country road, Cabot/André Jenny.*
BACK COVER: *Top row from left, Waterville, Alan L. Graham; Rutland, Caleb Kenna; Fairfield, Lynn M. Stone;*
second row, Bondville, David Middleton; Dorset, Kevin Bubriski; Berkshire, C.B. Johnson;
third row, Lake Fairlee, David A. Seaver; Camel's Hump, Alden Pellett; Green River Reservoir, André Jenny;
fourth row, Danby, Jerry LeBlond; Cambridge, Alan L. Graham; Weston, Paul Miller.

Printed in Canada. First printing.
Book design by Eugenie S. Delaney.
Photographs by *Vermont Life* contributing photographers.
Text by a selection of Vermont's finest writers.

Library of Congress Cataloging-in-Publication Data:
The 12 seasons of Vermont / photographs by Vermont Life contributing photographers;
text by a selection of Vermont's finest writers.
p. cm.
"A Vermont Life Book."
ISBN 1-931389-07-1
1. Vermont—Pictorial works. 2. Seasons—Vermont—Pictorial works. 3. Months—Pictorial works. 4. Natural
history—Vermont—Pictorial works. 5. Landscape—Vermont—Pictorial works. 6. Vermont—Description and travel.
7. Seasons—Vermont. 8. Months. 9. Natural history—Vermont. I. Title: Twelve seasons of Vermont. II. Vermont life.
F50.A613 2004
917.4304'44—dc22   2004012815

CONTENTS

AUTHORS

GARRET KEIZER *(January)* lives in Sutton with his wife and daughter. He taught public school for a number of years in the village of Orleans and was an Episcopal minister in Island Pond. He is the author of the essay collections *No Place But Here*, *A Dresser of Sycamore Trees*, and *The Enigma of Anger*, and of a novel, *God of Beer*. His fifth book, *Help: The Original Human Dilemma*, was published by HarperCollins in the fall of 2004. During the past several years, he has been a frequent contributor to *Harper's Magazine*.

JULIA ALVAREZ *(February)* is a poet (*The Woman I Kept to Myself*) and novelist (*How the Garcia Girls Lost Their Accents*, *In the Time of the Butterflies*). She grew up in the Dominican Republic but found her way to Vermont, where she is a writer-in-residence at Middlebury College. She divides her time between the tropical Champlain Valley and the green mountains of the Dominican Republic, where she and her husband, Bill Eichner, run a sustainable coffee farm and literacy center.

LELAND KINSEY *(March)* lives, works and writes poetry in Vermont's Northeast Kingdom with his wife and three children. He has five books in print, most recently *Sledding on Hospital Hill* and *In the Rain Shadow*. Every spring he helps in the family sugaring operation.

CHRIS BOHJALIAN *(April)* is the best-selling author of nine novels, including *Midwives*, *The Buffalo Soldier* and *Before You Know Kindness*. He lives in the Addison County town of Lincoln, from which he draws pieces of the Vermont fabric that plays a major role in his books.

HOWARD FRANK MOSHER *(May)* lives, writes and fishes in the Northeast Kingdom, which, he notes, to this day has a much larger population of brook trout than people. Most of his books, such as *Disappearances*, *A Stranger in the Kingdom* and *Where the Rivers Flow North*, have been set in northern Vermont. His newest is *Waiting for Teddy Williams*, a novel that combines his favorite literary locale, the fictional Kingdom County, with the star-crossed Boston Red Sox.

ELIZABETH INNESS-BROWN *(June)* is author of two collections of short stories. Her novel *Burning Marguerite* is set in the Champlain Islands, where she lives with her husband, Keith, and son, Michael. She teaches writing and directs the Writing Center at Saint Michael's College in Colchester, and although she has only lived in the state since 1987, her love affair with Vermont dates to a stay almost four decades ago, when she first saw the golden dome of the State House.

REEVE LINDBERGH *(July)* grew up in Connecticut, went to college in Massachusetts and in 1968 moved to Vermont, where she has been teaching, writing and living ever since. She has published numerous books on Vermont experiences for both children and adults. She lives near St. Johnsbury with her husband, writer Nathaniel Tripp, and their family.

KATHERINE PATERSON *(August)* is the author of more than 30 books, including 14 novels for young people. She has twice won both the Newbery Medal and the National Book Award and is the 1998 recipient of the most distinguished international award for children's

Dandelions in Cabot/Alan Jakubek.

literature, the Hans Christian Andersen Medal. In 1986 the Patersons moved to Barre Town, where they live on Trow Hill in a house built by John Trow for his son, Levi, in the 1830s. Vermont provides the setting for seven of her books. Her novel, *Jip, His Story*, set in pre–Civil War Vermont, was the first all-community read for the Barre area.

GALWAY KINNELL *(September)* has lived in Sheffield since 1961. The life around him in the Northeast Kingdom provides the subjects of many of his poems. He was Vermont State Poet from 1988 (when the first holder of the title, Robert Frost, posthumously but reluctantly relinquished his hold on it) to 1992. His *Selected Poems* won the Pulitzer Prize and the American Book Award in 1982.

CASTLE FREEMAN JR. *(October)* is the author of many essays, articles and reports concerning Vermont topics, including, most recently, the novel *My Life and Adventures*, published in 2002 by St. Martin's Press. He lives in Newfane.

DAVID BUDBILL *(November)* moved to Wolcott thirty-five years ago and, with his wife, the artist Lois Eby, bought land and built a house. Every year since he has cut a year's supply of firewood there, raised a year's supply of vegetables and written poetry, plays, essays and fiction. His narrative poems about people in an imaginary Vermont place called Judevine, a third world country within the United States, were collected in a book called *Judevine* (Chelsea Green, 1999). He made them into a play that has had 50 productions in 22 states. His next book will be *While We've Still Got Feet* (Copper Canyon Press, 2005).

NOEL PERRIN *(December)* has been a contributor to *Vermont Life* since 1963 and during 40 years of living in Thetford Center has become well-known for his thoughtful writing about rural life. Among his books are *Life with an Electric Car*, *First Person Rural* and *Amateur Sugarmaker*. The latter began as an article in *Vermont Life*.

INTRODUCTION

ALMOST EVERYONE KNOWS THAT Vermont has more than the usual four seasons. Four seasons may do perfectly well for other parts of the world, but the weather in Vermont simply gives us more.

For instance, there's that thawing time between late winter and early spring known as mud season, which is also, not coincidentally, roughly the same time as maple-sugaring season. And while most of the world thinks of autumn as a time of crisp apples and bright leaves, there's another, subtler fall after the bright leaves fall and before snow comes to stay that every Vermonter relishes. Then the landscape assumes somber tones of brown and purple, the chilly air smells of wood smoke, and we enter a season on the edge of winter for which there is no name other than November.

Every year is a cycle, regular though far from predictable, that echoes throughout the natural world in ways both obvious and subtle. Many Vermonters know that wild leeks are tastiest when they first poke up their green shoots through the dead-brown forest floor in April, and that tender crops like corn and green beans are at risk if planted

ABOVE: *Fall leaves, Underhill/Todd Cantwell.*
LEFT: *Danby Four Corners/André Jenny.*

much before Memorial Day. The late Governor Deane Davis, asked once when the best time to see fall foliage might be, replied without hesitation: "October 4." Davis' subtle joke was based on his bred-in-the-bone knowledge that the turning of the fall foliage is a deeply variable natural phenomenon, but the leaves are almost always good and bright by the first week in October.

How many seasons are there? It depends. The premise of this book is that in Vermont each month is distinctive enough to stand as a season of its own. The differences between months such as January and February are subtle, while the differences between months like April and May can be quite dramatic. But the differences are there, and to really appreciate life and nature here they need to be acknowledged and, ultimately, savored.

A Vermont summer is short, and seems shorter still when, after the wide, green expanse of July, August moves in with its shorter days and often-chilly nights, and harvest tables overflow with squash and sweet corn. The bitter cold of January mellows a bit in February, as does the winter light itself, catching new tones of pink and gold to temper

ABOVE: *A community quilt in Montgomery/Alden Pellett.*
LEFT: *Homemade skiing at Maplehurst Farm in Greensboro/Kindra Clineff.*

January's deep blue and giving subtle notice that the days are lengthening. The birds that sing their hearts out in May and June have become silent by July, save for a few ovenbirds and wood peewees; and the sound of newly open brooks splashing and gurgling beneath the snows are as much a part of March as spring peepers are of April.

Of course, Vermont's many seasons are never as neatly subdivided as we might like to make them and they don't correspond neatly to each month. Recently, in late March, I put on my backcountry skis and clambered up a mountain trail into a frozen alpine marsh called Beaver Meadow, ringed by the northern Green Mountains. The back roads were beginning to thaw and a thin layer of fresh mud anointed our car as we drove to our starting point. But after four miles of climbing with

Mount Mansfield from Underhill/André Jenny.

Apple orchard in Middletown Springs/Alan L. Graham.

a gain of more than a thousand feet in elevation, we found ourselves back in deep January, complete with a howling wind that pelted our numb hands and faces with flying snow. We skied down through six inches of fresh powder, then drove home over muddy roads, past rivers that had just cast off their winter carapace of ice.

ABOVE: *Luna moth in West Windsor/ Jacqueline Avery.*
RIGHT: *Waterbury Reservoir/ Jeb Wallace-Brodeur.*

Nevertheless, even accounting for Vermont's enormous environmental and climatological diversity, each month has its own particular character here, noted through the years by writers as different as Robert Frost, Dorothy Canfield Fisher and the contemporary novelist Howard Frank Mosher.

Since the distinction between months is often as much a feeling as it is a collection of scientific facts, for this book we asked a selection of

Vermont's finest writers to submit a short essay or poem related to their own experience of a favorite month. Their writings open each of the 12 chapters that follow. From Howard Frank Mosher's meditation on trout fishing in May to Garret Keizer's wry appreciation of deep January and Elizabeth Inness-Brown's celebration of June's colorful abundance, they give us their thoughts on the weather and seasons — something Vermonters have done for longer than Vermont has been a state.

What the accompanying photographs show us is nature's seasonal round, the changes that come to Vermont month-by-month, in a human context. Or perhaps the human beings are shown in a natural context. Whatever the emphasis, that's the way it is in Vermont — people and nature live, work and play together here. We are, after all, a part of nature, and we prosper when we stay close to and respect nature. Or so Vermonters have long believed.

The fact that nature here is often quite beautiful, whatever the month, doesn't hurt that relationship one little bit. ✑

— TOM SLAYTON
Editor-in-Chief, *Vermont Life*

JANUARY

by Garret Keizer

Y OU WOULDN'T THINK that extreme cold would have a sound, but it does, several in fact, one being that of a contracted nail popping out of the bedroom's outer wall like the shot of a gun.

You're awake — ready to hear the others that concur with the mercury: the aching creak of the snow underfoot, that crazy squealing from the speedometer cable (if you were lucky enough to start your car) while the needle jerks madly back and forth like an instrument calibrated to the end of the world.

LEFT: *Snowy road in Waterville/Alan L. Graham.*
ABOVE: *Bobwhite quail in Marlboro/John R. Ford.*

15

Since this is January, it may be that you watched *It's a Wonderful Life* last month, when you had Christmas to look forward to and the title didn't seem so ironic. In that case you may recall what the angel said: "Every time you hear a bell ring, it means that some angel's just got his wings." I know a middle-aged Vermonter who says, not without a certain misanthropic glee, that every time you hear a nail pop out of a house at thirty-five below, it means that another person has just decided to move to Florida.

Okay. I'm that man, and I was born in New Jersey. But to tell the truth, no time of year and no temperature ever make me feel so neighborly as I do now. I remember which people I ought to call and haven't called in a while: my friend with emphysema, who will not be running any errands today; the family whose lack of a basement means frozen pipes. No less important, I remember every person I can call if the car *doesn't* start — the farmer down the road; the friend with emphysema, who says I can always drive his.

Cold weather is the temperature of remembrance. January always comes like a little Lent. It reminds me of the things that start so automatically in the seasons of amnesia: the car, the water tap, the light bulb in the unheated shed. It reminds me that I am not God. "Let there be light," I say, flipping the switch, and there is no light.

ABOVE: *Lights on the snow, Calais/Paul O. Boisvert.*
RIGHT: *Hiker Bill Nash pauses on the snowy slopes of Mount Mansfield/Jim Westphalen.*

I am reminded of the deer huddled in the cedar swamp, of the stomping loggers close by (and thereby of how I got this paper), of the fuel truck drivers, who in their turn are forced to remember the people whose fuel assistance vouchers have run out. I talked to someone the other day who had misplaced his own compassion until the bitter cold reminded him to look for it in his wallet.

Most of all, the cold reminds me that I am mortal. The grave is supposed to be cold, though I doubt it's ever this cold. A thermometer placed six feet under the ground (ten feet counting the snow pack) could not register a wind-chill of fifty below. For a few moments, if I choose, I can open up my coat and feel colder than the dead, if only to remember that I am alive.

And that it is indeed a wonderful life.

After supper I work off my extra plate of spaghetti by throwing snow against the foundations of the house. I set the alarm for two a.m. to feed the furnace its second helping of wood.

In bed my wife and I cling to each other, castaways on a sea of icy sheets. We ask not for whom the nail popped — it wasn't for us. Not yet. "We won't be able to live here when we're old, you know," says she.

"Which means we're not old," say I, "because we're still here" — not a bad thought to have in the dark, as one foot pays court to another, through three pairs of socks. 🖋

16

JANUARY

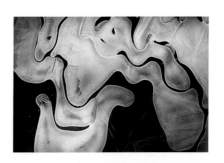

LEFT: *J. Maynard Miller walks toward the Bullock Farm in Guilford/Paul Miller.*

RIGHT: *Ice patterns in Lincoln/Brett Poirier.*

BELOW: *Waiting for a bite on the ice between West Swanton and East Alburg/Paul O. Boisvert.*

ABOVE: *Moonrise, sunset on Mount Mansfield/André Jenny.*

LEFT: *Common redpoll in Danby/David Middleton.*

FAR LEFT: *A cross-country skier glides by Middlebury College's Bread Loaf Campus in Ripton/ Caleb Kenna.*

FEBRUARY

by Julia Alvarez

THE JURY IS STILL OUT ON YOU,
February,
but it doesn't look good.

You start out with a hoax:
Groundhog's Day,
though everyone knows
six-plus weeks of winter await us
whether or not
the hog sees his shadow.

LEFT: *Craftsbury Outdoor Center/Paul O. Boisvert.*
ABOVE: *Snowboarder, sunset at Bolton Valley ski area/Dennis Curran.*

Mid-month you try again
with President's Day —
What kind of a holiday is that?

Who wants to think about
politics
in the dead of winter?

Finally, you end capriciously: a day or two
shorter
than any other month.

Your strategy: to keep us guessing;
to leap
or not to leap? that is your question.

Meanwhile, quietly, secretly,
you are plotting
a vast transformation . . .
Everything is happening
but nothing shows:
sap begins moving inside trees;

buds feel the first nudging; a hawk braves
the wind;
a black bear stirs in her cave;

foxes are searching for vixens;
chickadees gossip:
*the robins are coming, the robins
are coming!*

Everything is *not yet* and *almost;*
countdown begins
in the thin elms, in the frozen ponds.

ABOVE: *Sunrise lights a country road in Peacham/
Alan L. Graham.*
TOP: *Chickadee in West Dover/Michael Piniewski.*
RIGHT: *A Waterbury farm/Paul O. Boisvert.*

Stars change their positions:
the big dipper
scoops out longer days, shorter nights.

You fool us with blizzards,
subzero dawns,
ice storms to bend the birches,

long-bearded, white-haired wizard,
working magic,
you'll never get to enjoy.

Winter wimps, brats of the seasons
accuse you
of being a drag, an extra we don't need.

But what other month best teaches us
the invisible labor
that goes into any creation?

Anonymous worker, stonecutter
for the cathedrals
of summer, rough draft of the masterpiece

coming, guilty only of modesty —
we of the jury
find you innocent of all charges!

You are free to be the almost-end
of winter,
the not-yet beginning of spring.

ABOVE: *Ice boarding on Lake Champlain in South Hero/ Paul O. Boisvert.*

TOP LEFT: *Sliding fun in Rutland/ Caleb Kenna.*

BOTTOM RIGHT: *Signs of winter frustration in Barre/ Jeb Wallace-Brodeur, Barre-Montpelier* Times Argus.

BOTTOM LEFT: *A couple of winter enthusiasts, on a roll in Montpelier/ André Jenny.*

FAR RIGHT: *Snowboarder Travis Peckham heads for a soft landing on Mount Mansfield in Stowe/ Alden Pellett.*

ABOVE: *Templeton Farm in East Montpelier/André Jenny.*
RIGHT: *Birches in Reading/Alan L. Graham.*
FAR RIGHT: *Burke Hollow, filled with the colors of winter/Alan L. Graham.*

MARCH

by Leland Kinsey

MARCH LIES AT THE END of the hundred days, that one long season of almost unremitting cold, unique to the north country. Some certain sunny day though, from each of many alder bogs, osier wetlands, the first-of-the-year buzzy modern-telephone call of red-winged blackbirds will ring out — Oh, spring, sugaring, mud season.

As the month progresses, the sun's higher angle begins to laminate the snow into crusty layers with each new fall. March rains and freezes will add to the crust that tends to make this the

ABOVE: *Maple syrup grading bottles on a windowsill in Fairfield chronicle a sugaring season in miniature/Paul O. Boisvert.*
RIGHT: *Pitkin sugarhouse in Cabot/André Jenny.*

most difficult season for wild animals. Plants, animals and farmers are all finding out if the stores from summer and fall will be sufficient to pull them through. Since March holds records for snowfall, much new does fall, often in what's called *sugar snow*, flakes as big and easy-floating as

millers, those moths with dusty wings like a miller's clothes that hatch this time of year in great numbers. In the days of buckets instead of tubing, the millers had to be strained from the maple sap where they drowned by the thousands. The wet snow, often driven by spring winds, will sag the hearts of humans, but adds much to the quality and amount of the sweet-water sap that can be extracted from the dormant maples. Late in the month, winter's long grip easing, spring begins its fifteen-mile-a-day sweep north over Vermont after many weeks en route.

Vermont's brief local political season, centering on Town Meeting

ABOVE: *Sugarhouse in Cabot / Sandy Macys.*
TOP LEFT: *Drawing off syrup, Sheldon / Paul O. Boisvert.*
RIGHT: *Gathering sap the old-fashioned way in Fairfield / Lynn M. Stone.*

Day the first Tuesday in March, is also the traditional signal that those interested had better be ready for sugaring. Urban, suburban and rural sugaring amateurs will often hang a few buckets or jugs to make homemade syrup, usually of execrable quality, but mostly the sugar orchards nowadays are spider webbed with colorful tubing to capture the short season's liquid treasure. On days after a run, drivers will come upon tractors and trucks hauling sap to the sugarhouse tanks for the long days of boiling in, and steam plumes will dot the landscape, locating sugarhouses of those whose efforts keep the state number one in maple production.

The dirt roads that many Vermonters still live and commute on break up in March. The higher sun will sublime the ice and snow from south-facing hills first, but then all unshaded stretches of roads will be open and melting down to the deep-driven frost. Even paved highways will suffer the heaves and buckles caused by the frost, but portions of dirt roads will be like quicksand beds and plowed fields. Even solidified by overnight freezes, the roads' broken and rutted surfaces are difficult to drive, and on warm afternoons there's a certain grim joy to grinding through the thawed reaches.

March is often called the fifth season in Vermont, a month of seasons, difficult but promising, rich but hard. 🖋

ABOVE: *Stowe Hollow Covered Bridge/*
Alan L. Graham.

FAR LEFT: *A dirt road winds through Cambridge/*
Alan L. Graham.

TOP RIGHT: *Stuck in the mud in*
Barre Town/Sandy Macys.

BOTTOM RIGHT: *Lambing with Donny Joslin*
in Waitsfield/Sandy Macys.

BOTTOM LEFT: *The dangers of thin ice,*
Swanton/Paul O. Boisvert.

APRIL

by Chris Bohjalian

T HE POET T.S. ELIOT probably did not have Vermont in mind when he wrote that April was the cruelest month, but in all likelihood that was only because he never spent an April here. Spring certainly visits the Green Mountains in April, just as it does the more hospitable climes to the south . . . but it doesn't stay long. Crocuses emerge in the patches of vibrant green grass on our lawns, the sun high and the temperature flirting with seventy, only to be pummeled the next day by four or five inches of snow. Daffodils in Vermont

ABOVE: *The bicycling season opens in Woodstock/Rick Russell,* Vermont Standard.
RIGHT: *April in Washington/Alan L. Graham.*

must have a death wish. I have watched robins that have returned after a winter away huddle together on the talon-like branches of a hydrangea in the midst of an ice storm, at once incredulous and perturbed by the false advertising they saw writ large just the day before in the sky: A hot sun, a cerulean canopy, and a breeze that felt downright steamy.

This is, of course, the reason why April in Vermont can be cruel: The weather is fickle. Capricious. Unreliable. A real, sustained spring won't arrive here till the very last days of the month. In the meantime, we are teased. We are teased by precisely the sort of weather that causes the sugary sap to run fast in the maple trees — cold, sub-freezing nights followed by spectacularly balmy days. We are tempted into hauling our summer clothes out from the backs of our closets, only to find ourselves climbing (yet again) into our parkas and boots to shovel snow that is likely to be among the wettest and heaviest of the season.

Just how unpredictable is April? There is a sunrise service on Easter morning about a half-mile from my house, on a ridge in Lincoln with a postcard-perfect vista of Mount Abraham, one of the handful of Vermont peaks that top 4,000 feet. Some Easter mornings I have stood with the congregation on that hill in a blizzard, faith alone reassuring us that somewhere to the east the sun has indeed risen; other years I have stood there in a short-sleeve shirt, the moist grass causing my sneakers to squeak.

Vermonters are conditioned to expect the unexpected when it comes to April. What I find most interesting about the effect that weather has on attendance at the sunrise service is that it has none. Sunshine or snow, the people tromp up that hill Easter morning. This may say something about faith, but it may also say something about Vermonters.

After the storms and the cold and the long, dark nights that mark a Vermont winter, we don't mind the finicky persona of April. We'll endure a few more inches of snow and a couple of mornings with ice because they will, inevitably, be sandwiched between glorious tastes of the coming season. By the end of the month the first buds will be opening on those iconic sugar maples, the frogs will have rejoined the birds, and the days will stretch well beyond dinner.

Suddenly, it will be spring even here. 🖋

ABOVE: *Kingsbury Covered Bridge in South Randolph/John Knox.*
RIGHT: *Danby Four Corners/Allen Karsh.*

LEFT: *Maple Grove Farm sugarhouse in Williston/Kindra Clineff.*

MIDDLE: *Bromley Brook in Bondville/ David Middleton.*

FAR LEFT: *Covered bridge, Green River, Guilford/Allen Karsh.*

BELOW: *Camel's Hump State Forest in Huntington/Todd Cantwell.*

ABOVE: *By the time spring arrives, people get a little crazy: pond skimming at Sugarbush in Warren/Joanne Pearson.*

LEFT: *Potted tulips at the top of the single-chair lift at Mad River Glen in Fayston/Sandy Macys.*

RIGHT: *Grafton/Alan L. Graham.*

MAY

by Howard Frank Mosher

I N THE GREEN MOUNTAINS, May is the best month for brook-trout fishing. By then these brightly colored little native trout — more accurately, char — which inhabit nearly every spring-fed rill from the Canadian border to the Massachusetts state line, are ravenous. After five months of winter, they're ready to feed, and easy to catch.

In my corner of the state, the Northeast Kingdom, the streams are usually still icy-cold on May Day. But by the second week of the month, when the high hardwoods are yellowing

LEFT: *Barnet/André Jenny.*
ABOVE: *Walloomsac River in North Bennington/Harold Rowe.*

45

Spring mist rising from the Winooski River's North Branch near the village of Worcester/André Jenny.

with new leaves, it's finally time to reach for your favorite fly rod and head for the mountains.

Not, of course, that most Vermont brook-trout streams are suitable for fly casting. Take a look at the famous "Orvis Trout" picture of the leaping squaretail with the fly in the corner of its mouth. No doubt about it, the fish is a beauty. But where, in all that swampy bankside tangle, would you ever find room to cast a fly?

Nearly all the best old-time Northeast Kingdom fishermen I know

use "garden hackle" for bait. Brook trout seem unable to pass up a lively red angleworm, and worms are simple to fish.

A certain morning arrives. You'll recognize it immediately. The sugar-maple leaves will still be more gold than green. The sky, though mostly blue, will have a slight hazy softness. A real fisherman could no more stay out of the woods than the snow geese could stay south for the spring.

A Vermont brook in May is best fished upstream. Start where it crosses a dirt road and go all the way up to its source. That first tug-tug-tug at your worm will connect you all over again with the fish and the stream it lives in, with all your past Mays and with what, for me, is one of the best experiences Vermont has to offer. If you don't hurry, three or four miles of water will take the better part of a day. And you can take your pick of streams. Vermont has hundreds of them, many so small they aren't even named on topographical maps.

The character of most step-across-in-one-stride brooks changes three or four times from bottom to top. Near the road, you'll work your way through a disused pasture, past bright yellow cowslips or marsh marigolds, buttery trout lilies (note their speckled leaves), a patch of yellow coltsfoots.

Yellow seems to be the color of the season. Entering the woods, you'll see bankside yellow birch trees, pale gold in the sunlight, and maybe a bright yellow tiger swallowtail butter-fly drifting down the mountainside over the stream.

ABOVE: *Dandelions in Underhill/David A. Seaver.*
RIGHT: *Yellow lady's-slipper in Royalton/Judit Fabian.*

With luck, your brook will run through a little cedar bog with a fresh beaver dam. You'll most likely hear the water falling out of the dam before you see it. Here the trout may be slightly bigger. These days, though, for whatever reason — more roads, acid rain, clearcutting, some bad recent floods and droughts — a six-inch brookie is a good fish. Fried up crisp beside the stream with a little butter and salt, washed down with a cup of boiled coffee, it's hard to beat.

Higher up, there are woods violets, tiny yellow ones and white ones with lavender centers. There are white-and-pink spring beauties and deep-green moss and lacy ferns to put in your creel to keep your trout sweet and fresh. Here the trees may not have leafed out yet. Watch for the fiery orange throat of a Blackburnian warbler, which, in turn, had better keep a sharp eye out for a goshawk.

Finally, the brook turkey-tails out into three or four seeps too shallow for trout. Old snow, littered with hemlock needles, lies in the shadows of boulders broken off the mountain-top or dropped here ten thousand years ago by the same glacier that brought the ancestors of your fish.

Then it's evening and time to hike back down into May again, into a twilit meadow loud with the sleigh-bell jingling of the peepers, which you hear but almost never see except, occasionally, inside the gold-and-red belly of a brook trout. 🖋

LEFT: *Baseball in Charlotte/David A. Seaver.*
FAR LEFT: *Dandelion field in Wheelock/André Jenny.*
BELOW: *Plowing in Plainfield/*
Jeb Wallace-Brodeur, Barre-Montpelier Times Argus.

ABOVE: *Memorial Day Parade,
Vergennes/Alden Pellett.*
LEFT: *Colors blossom in Johnson/Alan L. Graham.*
RIGHT: *Tulips on parade, Dorset/Kevin Bubriski.*

JUNE

by Elizabeth Inness-Brown

W HEN JUNE FINALLY COMES, Vermont's lakes are high and blue, still fed by winter run-off. The trees are in full, sudden leaf, the woods moist and burgeoning, the black flies gathering, the mosquitoes hatching. From a distance, the mountains call, begging to be climbed — their trails dry at last, stony noses stuck up into the clear blue sky.

But however loud their voices, the garden calls louder.

For the gardener, June is the month of hope. The plants all in their rows, weeds temporarily vanquished, bugs momentarily

ABOVE: *Deer in summer grass/Paul Silver.*
RIGHT: *Station Covered Bridge in Cornwall/André Jenny.*

ABOVE: *Strawberries at the Brattleboro
Farmers' Market / Lois Moulton.*

LEFT: *The Strolling of the Heifers through downtown
Brattleboro / Kevin Bubriski.*

RIGHT: *Long Trail caretaker Daniela Molnar and Clover
atop windy Killington Peak / Alden Pellett.*

late. Only June is perfect for those seedlings, hair-thin roots seeking moisture. Time to pull radishes, snip the first, tender leaves of lettuce, pick strawberries, make a rhubarb pie.

And in the dewy morning, time to walk the flowerbeds. Forget-me-not. Viola. Jacob's Ladder. Columbine. *Campanula. Centaurea.* Spiderwort. Iris. June is the month of blue flowers.

The beards of the bearded iris are also called *falls.* And fall irises do. It's June when they bloom, heads so heavy that a heavy dew can bend them over. For two brief weeks, the warm breeze carries their sweet, peppery smell. Maybe this year, you think, it won't rain. But no — always in June, always just as the irises reach their peak, three or more blooms on a single stem, each big as an open hand — you wake to drenching rain. And with sinking heart, you know. Down they're coming, long green necks too weak to hold the wet heads. Petals melting, purple mush in the grass. In the morning you'll cut an armful and bring them into the house. What else can you do? They're irises, for heaven's sake. And for a moment, it's June.

at bay, everything green and healthy and *restrained* — perhaps this will be the ideal year, the year the flowers bloom well and in orderly sequence, the year nothing dies, the year we'll keep ahead of the weeds and bugs, the year the garden will be as we planned it, as we imagined it all winter.

A month is a long time in Vermont's garden season, but June — part May on one end, part July on the other — flashes by. So much to do, so little time. In go the tomatoes and basil, the ground finally ready for those plants we northerners demand despite their tropical ancestry. Before June, it's still too wet, too cool. After June, too dry, too hot, too

ABOVE: *Bluebird in East Dover/Michael Piniewski.*
TOP RIGHT: *Waterville/Kindra Clineff.*
RIGHT: *Haying in Starksboro/Paul O. Boisvert.*
FAR RIGHT: *Berkshire roadside/C.B. Johnson.*

LEFT: *Bike racing in Burlington/David A. Seaver.*

BELOW: *The Lake Champlain steamer* Ticonderoga *at the Shelburne Museum/Kindra Clineff.*

BELOW LEFT: *Chicken and child in Chester/Kathy Toris.*

RIGHT: *Champ, the Vermont Expos' mascot, cavorts on the dugout roof with a young fan at UVM's Centennial Field in Burlington/Dennis Curran.*

ABOVE: *Lady's-slippers in full bloom/C.B. Johnson.*
LEFT: *St. Johnsbury steeple/C.B. Johnson.*
FAR LEFT: *First cut of hay in Fletcher/Alan L. Graham.*

JULY

by Reeve Lindbergh

J ULY IS THE MONTH I DREAM ABOUT, in January, as the time when life on our farm is closest to perfection. The hay is ready to cut, homegrown vegetables are on the dinner table, my perennial garden is in full bloom. From daisies to delphiniums, the blossoming plants look self-confident and safe, and so they should. The danger of frost is behind them, along with the greater danger of annihilation by this blundering gardener.

I tend to yank up everything in sight early in the spring,

LEFT: *Haying on Cooper Hill in West Dover/Michael Piniewski.*
ABOVE: *A load of hay headed for the barn, Sheldon/Paul O. Boisvert.*

63

when seedlings are confusingly small. Still, much of my garden makes it through to glory in July. We also have hay in the fields and hollyhocks by the front door, head-high stalks bearing pink, white and magenta blossoms with diameters wider than the breadth of my palm. Hollyhocks grow so thickly by our stone steps that it can be a challenge to get into the house, but I refuse to thin their ranks. Any plant thriving in July has survived both me and the weather and deserves to live out its natural span.

Hay is another story. Hay needs cutting, and I look forward to this process every summer, probably because I don't have much to do with it. My husband tackles the hot and heavy work: cutting it, drying it and baling it. I come in at the end with my son and his friends, to help get it into the barn.

I like being in the fields, picking up the bales just after they drop from the baler and stacking them in piles to be collected later with the pick-up truck when we retrace the circle of tractor and baler around the field. I like putting the first layer of bales in the truck, always in the same position relative to the wheel wells, to make a strong base for the layers above. I like helping to build the fifty-four-bale hay cube, layer upon layer, sturdy and fragrant and swaying beneath us when we ride it down over the green curves of the land to the barn.

I wait up in the loft with the teenagers while my husband, on the ground floor, swings each bale off the truck and onto the pronged belt of the hay elevator. The bales clank their way to the high wooden platform above my head where my son stands, as other 16-year-olds in our family and in other families have stood before him. He throws the bales down through filtered beams of sunlight and hay dust to the loft, where his friends and I pick them up and stack them one more time, in great squared piles under the roof of the barn, for winter.

I know that January will return, the gardens will be gone and the curves of the hayfields cold and white. I realize that flowers and vegetables, hay and teenagers, seasons and lives, come and go. But I also know that like July on our farm, they will come again. So I keep right on dreaming. 🍂

ABOVE: *Sailing on Lake Champlain/Paul O. Boisvert.*
RIGHT: *Sunrise on Lake Bomoseen/André Jenny.*

LEFT: *The cornfields of the fertile*
Connecticut River Oxbow in Newbury/Alan L. Graham.
TOP RIGHT: *Bristol/Tom Pollak.*
BOTTOM RIGHT: *Crab spider on purple vetch/Gustav W. Verderber.*
BELOW: *Lupines and swallow in Waterville/Alan L. Graham.*

ABOVE: *Basin Harbor/Jean Carlson Masseau.*
FAR LEFT: *A leap into summer on Lake Fairlee/David A. Seaver.*
TOP LEFT: *The Charlotte–Essex ferry crossing Lake Champlain/Jeb Wallace-Brodeur.*
BOTTOM LEFT: *Sculling on Great Hosmer Pond in Craftsbury/Natalie Stultz.*

AUGUST

by Katherine Paterson

I F EVER IN THE DREARY DAYS of November or the
white wonderland of February or the mud of April you
forget that Vermont is the Green Mountain State, wait
until August. A ride from White River Junction to Burlington
on Interstate 89 is beautiful any time of year, but in August it
is a symphony in green. Unlike the upstart Rockies, Vermont's
mountains may be old and worn, but in the golden sun of
August, the canopy of variegated green on their slopes makes
them as welcoming as our grandmothers' laps.

ABOVE: *Handstand in the hay, Vergennes/Caleb Kenna.*
RIGHT: *Hiking the Long Trail, Camel's Hump/Alden Pellett.*

70

ABOVE: *Summer aroma, Shoreham/Natalie Stultz.*
LEFT: *Sunflowers in Shelburne/Paul O. Boisvert.*
RIGHT: *Route 5 along the Connecticut River just
north of the Newbury Oxbow/Alden Pellett.*

Sometimes it rains in August, and it seems unjust. Summer is so short in Vermont and you resent sitting huddled in the house, feeling cold and damp, unwilling to fire up the wood stove or turn on the furnace when it's still summer, for goodness sakes. You worry that the rain will drive away the tourists who come to see our beautiful mountains and swim in our icy lakes and breathe our pure mountain air. But when the sun shines, the hydrangeas are in full bloom, the tomatoes turn red, all is right with the world. Tomatoes fresh from the garden taste like no tomato east of Eden. You pull the cherry tomatoes from the vine and pop them, still warm from the sun, into your mouth. In a good August you make tomato sandwiches for lunch every day and tomato salad for dinner, but they are ripening so fast you chop up some to freeze against winter stews and even, a little reluctantly, share a few with the neighbors who have uncomplainingly taken uncounted zucchini off your hands.

You're never quite prepared when August starts to take her leave. Driving over the mountain you see a tree branch tinged in orange. It begins to get dark long before you want to go indoors. There is a chill in the air and the unmistakable smell of autumn. Your heart sinks. As magical as fall may be, it is hard to say goodbye to summer. You only hope the last giant tomato will ripen before an early frost blackens the plant. 🖋

ABOVE: *William Driscoll and his old Massey-Ferguson tractor, south of White River Junction/Alden Pellett.*

FAR LEFT: *Pedaling along the Ottauquechee River, Woodstock/Alan L. Graham.*

TOP RIGHT: *Summer snack/Paul Miller.*

RIGHT: *Louis Cheney and Bill Pinkham greet the morning traffic from the porch of Webster's snack bar and general store in McIndoe Falls/Alden Pellett.*

RIGHT: *Prize-winning gardeners, Craftsbury/Paul Rogers.*

BOTTOM RIGHT: *Joel Wright in the family barn, Bethel/Alden Pellett.*

FAR RIGHT: *Rick Wright, Joel's father, prepares for milking/Alden Pellett.*

BELOW: *David Mitchell and his Belgian work horse Mike in Lyndonville/Alden Pellett.*

Draft horses till the soil in Burlington's Intervale/Natalie Stultz.

ABOVE: *Silo and sunflowers/Kindra Clineff.*
LEFT: *Addison County Field Days/Alden Pellett.*

SEPTEMBER

by Galway Kinnell

BLACKBERRY EATING

I LOVE TO GO OUT IN LATE SEPTEMBER
among the fat, overripe, icy, black blackberries
to eat blackberries for breakfast,
the stalks very prickly, a penalty
they earn for knowing the black art
of blackberry making; and as I stand among them

ABOVE: *Deer Leap Preserve in Bristol/Todd Cantwell.*
RIGHT: *Mountain bikers roll along the
Sugarhouse Trail in Burke/Dennis Curran.*

LEFT: *Sunset, Killington Peak/Alden Pellett.*
RIGHT: *Green River Reservoir, Hyde Park/André Jenny.*
BELOW: *George D. Aiken Wilderness Area, Woodford/A. Blake Gardner.*

lifting the stalks to my mouth, the ripest berries
fall almost unbidden to my tongue,
as words sometimes do, certain peculiar words
like *strengths* or *squinched* or *broughamed*,
many-lettered, one-syllabled lumps,
which I squeeze, squinch open, and splurge well
in the silent, startled, icy, black language
of blackberry eating in late September. 🖋

ABOVE: *Fall games on Townshend Green/Paul O. Boisvert.*

FAR LEFT: *Littleton Long in his South Burlington orchard and,* RIGHT, *with his picking bag/both by Alden Pellett.*

FAR RIGHT: *Tunbridge World's Fair/Merlin Lacy.*

OCTOBER

by Castle Freeman Jr.

IN THE HEART OF THE HEART of the fall arrives a month that is, somehow, out of its time. By October, the tenth month, the year is old. The golden light of the afternoon partakes of age, and of a certain honest weariness and well-earned rest. But the curious thing about this long month is that it evokes not only the repose of age but also its devotion to memory, to the past. In October, as in no other month, the years, the decades fall away.

Nowhere is this more true than in the foothills and narrow

LEFT: *Country road in Cabot/André Jenny.*
ABOVE: *Fall leaves in Marlboro/Larry Richardson.*

valleys of Vermont. For two hundred years, Vermont was mostly a farm state, and its landscape was an agricultural landscape: open, well tended, domesticated. Over the past couple of generations, however, the state has been undergoing historic changes, in occupation, in settlement —

ABOVE: *Wood duck near Springfield/John R. Ford.*
RIGHT: *Playing in the leaves in Newfane/ Kindra Clineff.*
FAR RIGHT: *Tunbridge barn/John Sherman.*

and therefore a change, as well, in aspect. It's now a wilder, more wooded, less worked-over setting than it was.

Unquestionably, Vermont today is no longer a farm state in the way it was; but sometimes it still looks like one, it still feels like one, and never more than in this retrospective month. How it is we can hardly tell, but the sights and sounds of October, the October light, the October air, seem to restore the old agricultural order to the land, if only for a few weeks.

Take yourself for a drive on an October day, and see if you don't find

the same thing. On either hand, woodsheds are filled to their eaves, and more firewood is put up beside the houses in long, dun-colored stacks and walls. The big barns have a stuffed look, the look of abundance stored up. In reality, some of them are empty, and some have been turned to other uses, but in October even the obsolete barns have a fat and thriving look. They seem to have been transported back to the days when they meant business.

Across the intervale, three or four black-and-white cows in a pasture, half a dozen sheep on a rocky hillside, add to the landscape their familiar agrarian meaning. They preserve the memory of the millions of the same beasts that defined the state in the days when their kind had the people outnumbered ten to one.

Today, as in the centuries of Vermont's farming prime, October is, preeminently, the month of harvest. In our time, however, another, later harvest has come to follow the traditional harvest of the fields and mowings: I mean the gathering-in of the red and yellow leaves. By mid-October the leaves are down, and they lie in the woods, beside the roads, and among the houses in unimaginable numbers. Perhaps it's just because of this unfailing annual overflow that October is a month that seems to come out of the past. The crops, the stock, the old farm life, these things change. But the cycle of the year, which that life reproduces, does not change, and it has its image in the year's final gift, the bright harvest of the leaves. 🖋

88

ABOVE: *A walk along a maple-lined road in Peacham/André Jenny.*

LEFT: *Fall in Peacham/Merlin Lacy.*

ABOVE: *Elfin Lake, Wallingford/Todd Cantwell.*
RIGHT: *Pomfret/Alan L. Graham.*

LEFT: *Danby/Jerry LeBlond.*

TOP RIGHT: *Camel's Hump from Huntington/Alden Pellett.*

BOTTOM RIGHT: *Sheep in Ryegate/André Jenny.*

BELOW: *Fall colors in Hartford/John Sherman.*

LEFT: *Early morning fog on Marshfield Pond/André Jenny.*
RIGHT: *Bread Loaf Wilderness Area/A. Blake Gardner.*
BELOW: *Moose in Island Pond/John R. Ford.*

NOVEMBER

by David Budbill

J UST YESTERDAY THE WORLD let fall all the garments of
summer: heat, people, leaves. And birds — those faithless,
transitory, fly-by-nights — gone too.

Where do you enter a circle? When there is no beginning
where do you break in? Say November. Here. Enter through
the emptiness.

Sere gray. Sere brown. The bare trees, their skinny fingers
darkened by the rain, stretch against the sky. The earth is dank
and chill as an old deserted cellar. Overnight the world becomes

ABOVE: *Woodpile at the ready, Calais/Craig Line.*
RIGHT: *Underhill Center/Alan L. Graham.*

98

Two-Foot's old and well known lover standing naked, her arms folded around herself, shivering in the rain.

Heavy clouds and gray. Cold and spitting snow. Early November, the last geese going over low all morning. Their frantic cries of leaving fill him with a quiet joy. The world gets emptier, more barren, and he more alone.

ABOVE: *Frosted grass/David Middleton.*
RIGHT: *Mount Mansfield from Cambridge/Alan L. Graham.*

Done. His woodshed full of wood, his little house banked tight against the cold, the cellar full of meat and vegetables, Two-Foot comes inside and washes blood and summer from his fingernails. In silence now, in the dying year, in the darkening afternoon, he too darkens like these days. He watches stove light flicker. He sits and falls, as leaves fell, deeper into the coming dark, into the time of dream.

Stillness. Damp November calm. This relinquishing, giving in, gray turning toward winter, sweet melancholy, welcoming, opening, acceptance, receiving, this embrace of the quiet and the dark.

Deer season over. Deer hunters gone. Fewer and fewer people pass by on the road below the house. Chickadee — close, diminutive, silent — companion through the cold and dark, at the dooryard feeder again.

The next day he wanders aimless and alone in these barren, autumnal mountains everything, including him, dank with mists and full of darkness. Now toward home through the woods, through the chill rain. Popple and tamarack — the last leaves — down and sodden on the ground. All he can think about is how all too soon he too will be gone, and never will he walk again beneath these barren, rain-soaked trees, never will he pad again over these soft and quiet leaves, never return home again to stand beside the warming stove. He drinks deeply from this well, a sweet draught of melancholy.

Only a few coals remain in the stove. Build a new fire. Drink some tea. Cook a supper of rice and vegetables. Sit beside the stove. Listen to the silence of the night. Withdraw, return, pull in, to somewhere inside both house and life.

Bank on bank of clouds begin — like the folds of a shroud. Five o'clock. Almost dark. Chimney smoke lies down, crawls across the meadow like a slow soft snake. The sky steals light from both ends of the day. The long night steps slowly over the mountains.

ABOVE: *A touch of frost in Waitsfield/Dennis Curran.*
LEFT: *Screech owl and prey in Marlboro/John R. Ford.*
FAR LEFT: *Camel's Hump from Wind Gap, Duxbury/Jeb Wallace-Brodeur.*

DECEMBER

by Noel Perrin

ONE DULL WINTER EVENING a few years ago, I decided there were just two options open to me. One was to die of boredom. The other was to get out of the house. Naturally I chose that. The choice was made easier by the mild weather we were having. Though it was mid-December, temperatures stayed mostly in the 20s and 30s. There was no wind. Snow cover was only six or seven inches — of fluffy stuff that one could easily walk through, not worrying about snow-shoes or cross-country skis. Even the heavens were favorable;

LEFT: *Weston mill/Paul Miller.*
ABOVE: *Red fox/David Middleton.*

105

the well-over-half moon was riding high, and sending down a chilly but usable light. Perfect conditions for a woods walk.

Here was my plan, my simple plan: I would do an explore. That is, I'd walk in a direction I had never walked in before. In my case that happened to be north, which I thought sounded rather romantic.

As it turned out it *was* romantic, though not in the way I had imagined. Here's what happened. I left my house about fifteen minutes after supper, and walked straight into a piece of enchanted forest. That is, I stumbled into a glade full of enormous trees. I counted twelve. Ten were in a row along what must once have been a fenceline, and two were up near a cellarhole. All were just plain huge. It is not easy to tell what kind of tree you are dealing with just by looking at the bark (no leaves in

ABOVE: *Snowshoeing in Bolton/Alden Pellett.*
LEFT: *Ski-skating in Craftsbury/André Jenny.*
RIGHT: *Killington Peak/David Middleton.*

December) and it's even harder if your only source of light is a two-thirds moon. But I knew with a fierce certainty that these were sugar maples. My guess is that some farmer planted them between 1800 and 1850, which makes them pre-Civil War trees.

All right, these trees are big and they are old. They could certainly be tapped for making maple syrup — if they were in a convenient location, which they are not. But enchanted? What makes them that? Several things, of which I'll cite just two.

One is the role these giant trees play in the life of the glade. They're at least a century older than any other tree there, and to a human mind it comes natural to see them as protectors and guardians, as they would be in a fairy tale. In certain moods I can imagine their having the ability to stop a chainsaw.

Secondly there's the question of beauty. All healthy trees (and some sick ones) have at least a measure of beauty, but these 12 maples have a double share. They do on moonlit nights when there's snow on the ground, anyway. Each of them casts a shadow which almost perfectly replicates its foliage. There is something magical about it.

But then, there's something magical about trees altogether. Ask any druid. 🖋

ABOVE: *Taking flight at Jay Peak/Alden Pellett.*
FAR LEFT: *Jeff Hill sends the powder*
flying on Mount Mansfield/Paul O. Boisvert.
LEFT: *Rob Frost climbs an icy wall in Smugglers Notch/Alden Pellett.*
TOP: *Super tubing in Newport/Paul O. Boisvert.*

ABOVE: *Calvary Episcopal Church in Jericho/André Jenny.*

FAR LEFT: *A musher and his team round a corner at the Craftsbury Outdoor Center/Elinor Osborn.*

LEFT: *A sleigh ride at Mountain Valley Farm, Waitsfield/ Dennis Curran.*

BOTTOM: *Flag and snow in Norwich/Jon Gilbert Fox.*

RIGHT: *Chris and Megan Howard bring home the tree in Bakersfield/Paul O. Boisvert.*

BELOW: *A sleigh cuts through the snow at the annual Wildflower Inn Sleigh Rally in East Burke/Jon Gilbert Fox.*